SUZANNE COLLINS

Author of the
HUNGER GAMES
TRILOGY

by Melissa Ferguson

Snap
books

CAPSTONE PRESS
a capstone imprint

Snap Books are published by Capstone Press,
1710 Roe Crest Drive, North Mankato, Minnesota 56003
www.mycapstone.com

Cataloging-in-Publication Data is on file with the Library of Congress.
ISBN 978-1-5157-1326-5 (library binding)
ISBN 978-1-5157-1334-0 (paperback)
ISBN 978-1-5157-1338-8 (eBook PDF)

To my parents, Kathy and Jim. Your support means the world.

Editorial Credits
Abby Colich, editor; Bobbi Wyss, designer;
Kelly Garvin, media researcher; Laura Manthe, production specialist

Photo Credits
Alamy/H.S. Photos, 18; Newscom: Abaca Press SIPA, 5, Album, 23 (bottom),
Consolidated Hector Robertin/picture-alliance/dpa, 7, Jeff Malet Photography, 20, Mario
Anzuoni/Rueters, 27, RE/Westcom/starmaxinc.com, 29, World History Archive, 9 (top);
Shutterstock: 89studio, 19, 23, Asillsem, 8, dezi, 22, fluke samed, cover, 1, Georgii
Shipin, 13, Inga Linder, 9 (b), Jaguar PS, 25, Konstantin Chagin, 19 (b), KUCO, 17,
Natykach Nataliia, 10, Oleg Golovnev, 12, Photographee.eu, 15, Songquan Deng, 11,
zukerka, 19 (top)

Printed in China.
007736

TABLE OF CONTENTS

A Writer on Fire

Suzanne Collins was living her dream. She was working as a writer for several TV shows at Nickelodeon in New York City. Then a friend encouraged her to try something new.

That encouragement led Suzanne to write a children's book in 2003. About a boy and a fantasy underground world, *Gregor the Overlander* launched Suzanne's career as a best-selling writer.

After *Gregor the Overlander,* Suzanne wrote one book a year for the next four years. She finished the Underland Chronicles in 2007. Then in 2008 she wrote the first book in the **series** that would make her famous—*The Hunger Games.*

WRITING TO STARDOM

The Hunger Games was a **phenomenon**. It soared to the top of best-seller lists. Readers were buzzing. In 2009 and 2010, Suzanne published *Catching Fire* and *Mockingjay*. The **trilogy** has sold more than 65 million copies in just the United States.

For Suzanne writing isn't about the money or fame. It's about creating stories that ignite her readers' imaginations. With her books flying off shelves and into the hands of readers of all ages, Suzanne is a writer on fire.

series—a number of things coming one after another

phenomenon—something very unusual or remarkable

trilogy—a series of three literary works that are related and follow the same story or theme

Suzanne Collins

Growing Up Military Style

Suzanne was born in Connecticut in 1962 to Michael and Jane Collins. She had three older siblings—Kathy, Jeanie, and Drew. Her dad was an officer in the U.S. Air Force. Because of his position in the military, the family moved a lot.

YEAR OF CHANGES

In 1968 the Collins family packed up and moved to Indiana. It was a year of big changes. Six-year-old Suzanne had to get used to living in a new place. Then her dad left to fight in the Vietnam War (1959–1975).

Suzanne missed her dad. Sometimes she would see images of the war on TV. She was too young to understand the dangers he faced. Still, she worried about him being so far away.

When Suzanne's father returned, he talked openly to his children about what he had seen. He told them about the consequences of war, such as fear, loss, and death. Her dad had many nightmares after he came home. This made Suzanne anxious. Later, war would become a main **theme** in her books.

theme—a central idea that a story addresses

Children of those in the military move on average six to nine times between kindergarten and grade 12.

members of the United States Army in Vietnam, 1969

THE NEXT MOVE

When Suzanne was 11, the family moved again. This time it was across the Atlantic Ocean to Brussels, Belgium.

Suzanne adjusted to life in Europe. She enjoyed exploring the continent's many battlefields and castles with her family. Michael Collins taught his children about the history of these places. Once the family visited a field of red poppy flowers. Michael reminded his children that although the field was pretty to look at, many soldiers had died there. The way he spoke made Suzanne feel as if she was traveling back in time.

HOOKED ON READING

In Belgium Suzanne attended a school for American children. Her favorite teacher was Miss Vance, who taught English. Miss Vance read stories to her class that are not usually told to kids Suzanne's age. One was the **short story** "The Tell-Tale Heart" by Edgar Allan Poe. In this scary tale, the main character murders an old man and buries him under the floorboards. Later, the murderer begins to hear the heartbeat of the man he killed. The stories Miss Vance shared with her class helped Suzanne get hooked on reading.

Edgar Allan Poe

short story—a short piece of fiction with few characters and one event

SUZANNE'S BOOKSHELF

Curious to know what books Suzanne read when she was your age? These were some of her favorites:

* *A Wrinkle in Time* by Madeleine L'Engle
* *Myth and Enchantment Tales* by Margaret Evans Price
* *A Tree Grows in Brooklyn* by Betty Smith
* *The Phantom Tollbooth* by Norton Juster

CHAPTER 3

Becoming a Writer

As she was set to start high school, Suzanne and her family moved back to the United States. She enrolled at the Alabama School of Fine Arts in Birmingham. Suzanne graduated in 1980. Then she attended Indiana University. Suzanne studied to become an actor. She had fun performing in plays. Later she realized that she wanted to create her own words.

THE BIG APPLE

Suzanne moved to New York City in 1987. There she earned a master's degree in dramatic writing from New York University.

With her master's degree in hand, Suzanne began working as a writer for children's TV. She was a talented storyteller. Suzanne filled her scripts with action and adventure. She brought this talent to TV programs such as *Clarissa Explains It All* and *Wow! Wow! Wubbzy!* at Nickelodeon.

Suzanne developed skills working for TV, including writing **dialogue**. These skills would help her in her next big writing adventure.

dialogue—the words spoken between two or more characters

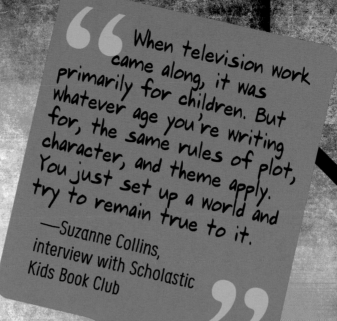

"When television work came along, it was primarily for children. But whatever age you're writing for, the same rules of plot, character, and theme apply. You just set up a world and try to remain true to it.

—Suzanne Collins, interview with Scholastic Kids Book Club

New York City

GREGOR THE OVERLANDER

In the early 2000s, Suzanne worked on the children's TV show *Generation O!* One of Suzanne's coworkers noticed her gift for storytelling. He encouraged her to ditch TV and write her own book.

Suzanne followed his advice. Several things around Suzanne inspired her writing. One story was Lewis Carroll's *Alice in Wonderland*. In this tale a girl falls down a rabbit hole into a magical, underground world.

illustration *from* Alice in Wonderland *by Lewis Carroll*

Ideas also came to Suzanne while she was wandering the streets of New York City. What if someone fell down a manhole? What kind of world might be found beneath the streets of the city?

Suzanne imagined a boy named Gregor. Gregor tumbles into the Underland, an underground society where humans live amongst giant, creepy-crawly critters. Suzanne began work on what would become her first book, *Gregor the Overlander*.

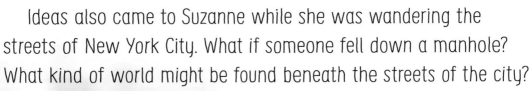

✔ FACT

Suzanne spent time learning about spiders, bats, cockroaches, and rats. She wanted to better understand these creatures to describe them to readers. The bat was her favorite animal to research.

GETTING PUBLISHED

Suzanne edited and revised *Gregor the Overlander* for several months. Then she began the process of looking for a **publisher**. First she contacted **literary agent** Rosemary Stimola.

Rosemary read Suzanne's story. She couldn't put it down. She sent the **manuscript** to Scholastic, a major children's book publisher. Scholastic released *Gregor the Overlander* in 2003.

After *Gregor the Overlander*, Suzanne wrote four more books for what would become The Underland Chronicles. *Gregor and the Prophecy of Bane*, *Gregor and the Curse of the Warmbloods*, *Gregor and the Marks of Secret*, and *Gregor and the Code of Claw* completed the series.

Soon after finishing The Underland Chronicles, Suzanne wrote a picture book. *When Charlie McButton Lost Power* came out in 2005. The main character, Charlie McButton, plays only computer games. One day he's faced with a dilemma when the electricity goes out.

publisher—a company that makes and sells printed things such as newspapers or books

literary agent—someone who helps a writer find a publisher

manuscript—a written document

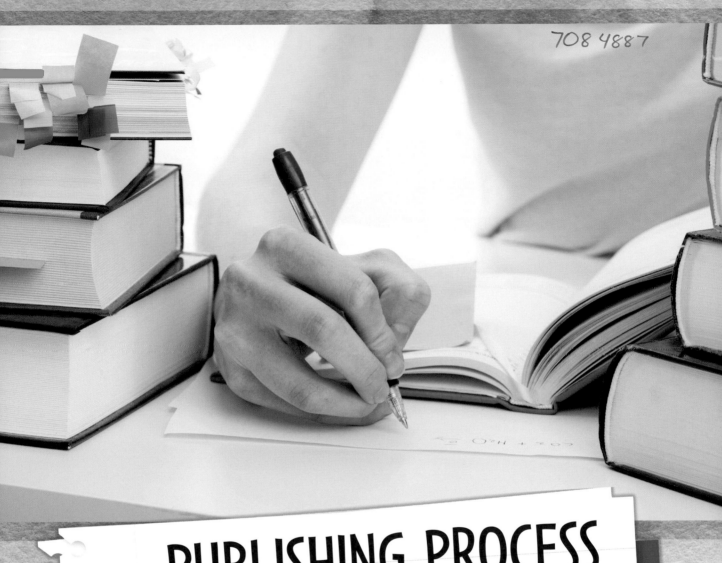

PUBLISHING PROCESS

Getting a book published can be a long process. After an author finishes a manuscript, he or she begins looking for an agent. The author may need to send writing samples to several agents before one agrees to represent him or her. Then the agent begins looking for a publisher. Several publishers may look at the manuscript before it is accepted. Publishers and agents negotiate on how much the author will get paid. The author may need to make several revisions to the manuscript before it is ready to be published.

CHAPTER 4

The Hunger Games

Suzanne's inspiration for her next book was fitting for a TV writer. It came one night while she was watching a reality show. Suzanne changed the channel to a news story on the Iraq War (2003–2011). The two images—reality TV and real-life war—blended together in her mind. This image became the basis for *The Hunger Games*.

HUNGER STORIES

Her dad's tales of growing up during the Great Depression (1929–1939) also influenced Suzanne. In these years many people could not find jobs. Food was scarce. Suzanne's dad hunted for meat. He gathered plants to help feed his family.

Suzanne used this to create the setting for District 12 in *The Hunger Games*. The people of District 12 are hit by hard times. Like Suzanne's father, the **protagonist** Katniss Everdeen must hunt and search for food in the wilderness to survive.

THESEUS AND THE MINOTAUR

Another inspiration for the *The Hunger Games* was the Greek **myth** *Theseus and the Minotaur*. In this story young children are sent into a maze. There a monster is waiting to eat them. Theseus, the prince of Athens, volunteers to enter the maze. He fights the monster, defeating it. He becomes the hero. Suzanne has compared Katniss to Theseus.

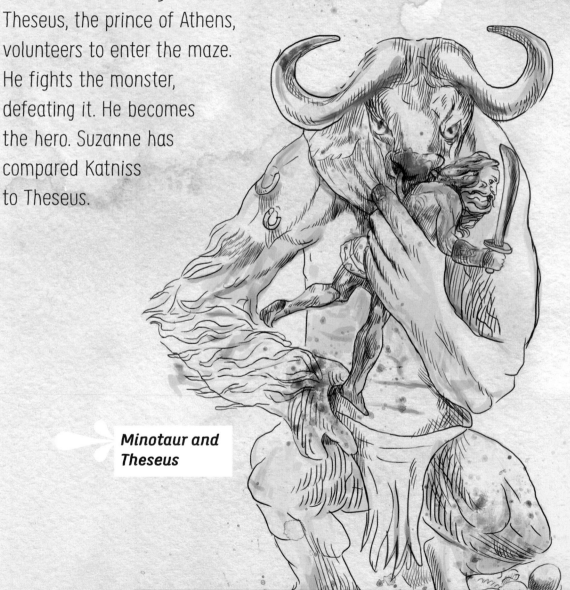

Minotaur and Theseus

protagonist—the main character in a play or book
myth—a story from ancient times

A DYSTOPIAN STORY

For *The Hunger Games*, Suzanne created the **dystopian** society of Panem. In Panem there are 12 districts. A strict government in the Capitol rules the districts. The people of the Capitol live like movie stars. Their dazzling lifestyle is very different from the people of the districts, who are poor, hungry, and **oppressed**. Every year ceremonies called reapings take place across Panem. At the reapings each district draws the name of two children (a boy and a girl). The children are then forced to fight one another to the death on TV. The winner of the Hunger Games is the last person to survive. The winner's district receives wealth and riches for the next year.

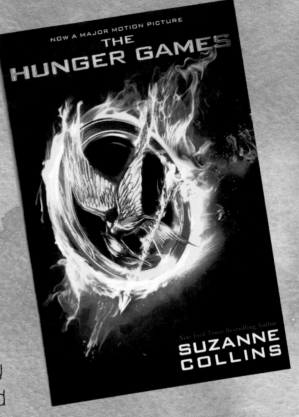

The book's **narrator** is the brave and strong-willed Katniss Everdeen. Katniss becomes a contestant in the Hunger Games when she volunteers to take her sister's place after her name is drawn in a reaping.

dystopian—a dangerous and bleak world likely created by a catastrophic event such as a virus outbreak or nuclear war

oppressed—treated in a cruel and unjust way

narrator—a person who tells a story or describes an event

RESEARCH FIRST

Before Suzanne begins tapping away on her laptop, she digs into the research for her story. This allows her to be sure that what she is writing is accurate. Suzanne read a stack of books about outdoor survival skills before writing *The Hunger Games*.

Suzanne at a book signing for Mockingjay

A SMASH HIT

From the moment it hit bookshelves in 2008, *The Hunger Games* tore up the charts. Word spread like wildfire that this was the "it" book. Readers—both teens and adults—turned the pages with lightning speed. The novel quickly topped best-seller lists.

After *The Hunger Games*, readers scrambled to get their hands on the next books in the series. Would Katniss and the people of Panem survive a war against the Capitol?

In 2009 Scholastic released *Catching Fire*. In *Catching Fire* readers follow Katniss as she returns home after the Hunger Games. A rebellion against the Capitol is brewing in the districts. Katniss becomes a symbol of the revolution.

One year later the final book in the series, *Mockingjay*, was published. The story concludes with Katniss and her supporters waging a major battle against the Capitol.

"I think people bring a lot of themselves to the book. When *Hunger Games* first came out, I could tell people were having very different experiences. It's a war story. It's a romance. Other people are like, it's an action adventure story ... for me it was always first and foremost a war story, but whatever brings you into the story is fine with me."

—Suzanne Collins, interview with *TIME* magazine, November 22, 2013

RESPONDING TO CRITICISM

Despite its brilliant success, the Hunger Games series faced some backlash. Not everyone liked the books. Suzanne's writing came under fire for being too violent. Critics said her themes of war and killing were too dark for young readers.

Throughout the series Suzanne includes scenes that show young people fighting to the death. War is portrayed with the tragic killing and wounding of innocent lives. Because of this content, some parents thought that the books should not be allowed in schools.

Suzanne disagrees with this criticism. She listened to her dad's war stories from an early age. As a child Suzanne learned to think critically about the world around her. She says that young people should not be sheltered from the reality of war. Suzanne believes that when children are old enough, they should be taught what war really means.

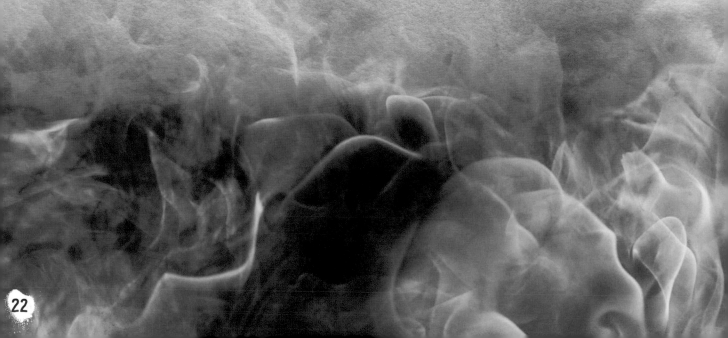

BATTLE ROYALE

The Hunger Games is often compared to the Japanese novel-turned-film *Battle Royale*. Written by Koushun Takami in 1999, *Battle Royale* tells the story of Japanese schoolchildren who are taken to an island as part of a government-controlled program. They are given weapons and then forced to kill one another until only one student is left alive. Some people think that Suzanne copied her story from *Battle Royale*. Suzanne says that she has never read the book.

a scene from the Japanese film Battle Royale

CHAPTER 5

Hollywood Calls

Filmmakers soon took notice of the hype surrounding *The Hunger Games*. Producers wanted to create a movie version of the book. No one knew the characters and the story better than Suzanne. She wanted to participate in choosing a director and casting the actors. It was important to her that the books came to life in the right way.

Suzanne also helped write the **screenplay**. Her experience as a TV writer came in handy. When readers heard about the plans for a movie, many jumped online to discuss who they thought should play each character.

MOVIE FEVER

In 2011 Suzanne announced that Jennifer Lawrence would star as Katniss Everdeen. The film would also star Josh Hutcherson as Peeta and Liam Hemsworth as Gale.

Fans went wild for *The Hunger Games* movie. The film came out on March 23, 2012. It made a whopping $155 million its first weekend. The equally popular *Catching Fire* followed the next year. The final book, *Mockingjay*, was split into two movies.

screenplay—the written version of a movie or TV show

Jennifer Lawrence received training in archery prior to movie filming. Katniss uses a bow and arrow in *The Hunger Games*.

actors Josh Hutcherson, Jennifer Lawrence, and Liam Hemsworth at The Hunger Games *film premier in 2012*

IN THE SPOTLIGHT

Celebrity is not something Suzanne craves. She enjoys talking about her books. However, she is very protective of her privacy. With the media wanting interviews and fans excited to meet her, keeping a low profile is tough.

Since *The Hunger Games* became an instant sensation in 2008, Suzanne has been involved in a flurry of TV appearances and book tours. People on the street want to take her picture and get her autograph. After the release of the movies, the hype surrounding Suzanne became even greater.

This is all very exciting for Suzanne, but also concerning. She doesn't like a lot of media attention. She limits the number of interviews she does. She also doesn't give much personal information about herself or her family. She wants the focus to remain on her writing.

Suzanne signs autographs during the movie premier of Catching Fire.

✔ FACT

TIME magazine named Suzanne Collins one of the 100 most influential people in 2010.

CHAPTER 6

What's Next?

Suzanne's most recent children's book, *Year of the Jungle: Memories from the Home Front*, came out in 2013. This picture book follows a young girl whose dad leaves to fight in the Vietnam War. It's based on Suzanne's own experiences. Suzanne hopes this story will help children whose parents have been to war.

LIFE TODAY

Suzanne lives in Connecticut with her husband and two kids. She continues to write. Occasionally, she makes appearances to promote her books.

Through her writing Suzanne has motivated readers of all ages to pick up a book and become lost in the story. Whatever Suzanne has planned next, it's sure to keep readers captivated. Perhaps it will inspire them to write stories of their own.

> " A lot of people tell writers to write about what they know. And that's good advice, because it gives you a lot of things to draw on. But I always like to add that they should write about things that they love ... things that fascinate or excite them.
>
> —Suzanne Collins interview with *Scholastic Teacher* "

Glossary

dialogue (die-uh-LOGG)—the words spoken between two or more characters

dystopian (diss-TOH-pee-uhn)—a dangerous and bleak world likely created by a catastrophic event such as a virus outbreak or nuclear war

literary agent (LIT-uhr-air-ee AY-juhnt)—someone who helps a writer find a publisher

manuscript (MAN-yoo-skript)—a written document

myth (MITH)—a story from ancient times

narrator (NARE-at-err)—a person who tells a story or describes an event

oppressed (oh-PRESSED)—treated in a cruel and unjust way

phenomenon (fe-NOM-uh-non)—something very unusual or remarkable

protagonist (proh-TAG-uhn-ist)—the main character in a play or book

publisher (PUHB-lish-er)—a company that makes and sells printed things such as newspapers or books

screenplay (SKREEN-play)—the written version of a movie or TV show

series (SIHR-eez)—a number of things coming one after another

short story (SHORT STOR-ee)—a short piece of fiction with few characters and one event

theme (THEEM)—a central idea that a story addresses

trilogy (TRILL-uh-jee)—a series of three literary works that are related and follow the same story or theme

Read More

Grundell, Sara. *FAME: Suzanne Collins*. Vancouver: Bluewater Productions, 2012.

Kopp, Megan. *Suzanne Collins*. New York: AV2 by Weigl, 2013.

Wheeler, Jill C. *Suzanne Collins*. Children's Authors. Minneapolis: ABDO Publishing Company, 2013.

Internet Sites

FactHound offers a safe, fun way to find Internet sites related to this book. All of the sites on FactHound have been researched by our staff.

Here's all you do:

Visit *www.facthound.com*

Type in this code: 9781515713265

Check out projects, games and lots more at
www.capstonekids.com

Critical Thinking Using the Common Core

1. Name one thing that led Suzanne to go from TV writer to best-selling book author. (Key Idea and Details)

2. Suzanne's father's experiences fighting in the Vietnam War influenced her writing. Do you think Suzanne's stories would be different if her father hadn't fought in the war? Why or why not? (Integration of Knowledge and Ideas)

3. Reread the text on page 26 and look at the photo. What feelings do you think Suzanne had while this photo was being taken? (Craft and Structure)

Index